LEMONS

LEMONS
A BOOK OF RECIPES

HELEN SUDELL

LORENZ BOOKS

First published in 2014 by Lorenz Books
an imprint of Anness Publishing Limited
108 Great Russell Street, London WC1B 3NA
www.annesspublishing.com
www.lorenzbooks.com; info@anness.com

A CIP catalogue record for this book is available from The British Library

Publisher Joanna Lorenz
Editorial Director Helen Sudell
Designer Nigel Partridge; Illustrations Anna Koska

Photographers: Martin Brigdale, Steve Moss, William Lingwood, Craig Robertson, Charlie Richards, Gus Filgate, Simon Smith, Frank Adam, John Whitaker, Nicki Dowey, Jake Eastman
Recipes by: Matthew Drennan, Ghillie Basan, Marlena Spieler, Rena Salaman, Brian Glover, Janny de Moor, Rebekah Hassan, Jenny White, Christine Ingram, Jeni Wright, Sunil Vijayakar, Sara Lewis, Maggie Mayhew, Joanna Farrow, Ann Nicol, Coralie Dorman, Catherine Atkinson, Annette Yates, Claire Ptak, Valentina Harris, David Jones

Printed and bound in China

COOK'S NOTES

· Bracketed terms are intended for American readers.

· For all recipes, quantities are given in both metric and imperial measures and, where appropriate, in standard cups and spoons. Follow one set of measures, but not a mixture, because they are not interchangeable.

· Standard spoon and cup measures are level. 1 tsp = 5ml, 1 tbsp = 15ml, 1 cup = 250ml/8fl oz.

· Australian standard tablespoons are 20ml. Australian readers should use 3 tsp in place of 1 tbsp for measuring small quantities.

· American pints are 16fl oz/2 cups. American readers should use 20fl oz/2.5 cups in place of 1 pint when measuring liquids.

· Electric oven temperatures in this book are for conventional ovens. When using a fan oven, the temperature will probably need to be reduced by about 10–20°C/20–40°F. Since ovens vary, you should check with your manufacturer's instruction book for guidance.

· The nutritional analysis given for each recipe is calculated per portion (i.e. serving or item), unless otherwise stated. If the recipe gives a range, such as Serves 4–6, then the nutritional analysis will be for the smaller portion size, i.e. 6 servings. The analysis does not include optional ingredients, such as salt added to taste.

· Medium (US large) eggs are used unless otherwise stated.

PUBLISHER'S NOTE

CONTENTS

INTRODUCTION

With their distinctive shape and cheerful colour, lemons give us one of life's great flavours. They are an indispensable kitchen standby: few other ingredients have lemon's ability to enhance sweet and savoury dishes.

Lemons are inseparable from the image of the countries surrounding the Mediterranean, but they probably came originally from the East Indies. The Romans considered them to be a luxury; when the Roman empire collapsed, lemon cultivation did too. The Moors planted them again in the Sahara, Andalusia and Sicily from the eighth century on. Columbus took them to America and it was on long sea voyages where scurvy was rife that it was finally realised that the disease, caused by a deficiency of vitamin C, could be cured by eating citrus fruit.

Below: Grating lemon results in a soft paste.

Above: Lemon tea with honey is very soothing.

HEALTHY PROPERTIES

As well as the vital vitamin C contained in lemons, they are also are an excellent source of bioflavonoids, which have antioxidant properties that help maintain the immune system and protect against disease, including some cancers. They also contain small amounts of the minerals potassium, calcium and phosphorus. A famous antiseptic, lemon juice soothes sore throats, especially when combined with a spoonful of honey in a warm drink. It is also thought that lemon can help relieve rheumatism.

COOKING WITH LEMONS

All dishes, both sweet and savoury, benefit from the distinctive tang of lemon. It is seldom served solo, but rather it is used primarily to enhance or flavour other foods.

Lemon juice will tenderize meat in a marinade, give fresh cream a soured taste, and prevent fruit and vegetables –

especially apples, celeriac, artichokes, avocados and potatoes – from oxidizing and browning. It also makes a great marinade for both fish and shellfish, but do not marinate for more than an hour or the juice will start to "cook" or denature the protein. The juice can feature as the principal flavouring in such dishes as lemon mousse or cheesecake, or as a complementary flavour, for example, in a lemon mayonnaise or cake frosting.

Below: A cannelle knife is used to make fine julienne strips.

However, it is the skin of the lemon that holds the really powerful flavouring ingredient. If you rub a lump of sugar over the surface of a lemon it will soak up the aromatic oil. Use the sugar in a dessert sauce or cocktail, and it will add a subtle citrus flavour. Grated or pared lemon rind tastes wonderful in cakes, desserts and even savoury dishes, such as beef, lamb, pork or chicken casseroles. When paring or grating lemons, take care not to include any of the pith, which is unpleasantly bitter. Where the pith is useful is in helping jam to set, since it contains a lot of pectin, as do the pips (seeds).

Preserved lemons feature in both sweet and savoury recipes. Sliced or quartered lemons, preserved in salt and stored in olive oil are widely used in North African cooking, especially in chicken and fish dishes. Candied lemon slices or half slices may be used to decorate creamy iced desserts and tarts.

Above: Candied lemon slices make appealing decorations.

Slices or wedges of lemon are classic garnishes for hot and cold fish and shellfish dishes. They are also natural partners for chicken and veal and the favourite decoration to adorn a cocktail glass.

Finely grated lemon rind may be sprinkled over sweet and savoury dishes and, when combined with finely chopped flat leaf parsley and garlic cloves, it forms an Italian garnish called gremolata, often used with roast meats.

USING LEMONS

PEELED RIND
This is added to stocks to give a lemon flavour and to counteract any greasy aftertaste. It is discarded after cooking.

GRATED LEMON RIND
Sometimes called zest, this can be grated finely or coarsely, according to your recipe requirements. Coarsely grated rind can be added to soups, certain savoury dishes and puddings where a lemony flavour is required. It is particularly good added to chicken and duck recipes, in curries and in rich stews, again to counteract any greasiness and enhance flavour. Finely grated rind similarly adds a subtle lemon flavour to desserts and is suitable for sauces, cakes, ice creams and sorbets.

JULIENNE STRIPS
An alternative and pretty decoration for a variety of sweet and savoury dishes.

WEDGES AND SLICES
Used for garnishing and serving. Lemon wedges tend to be served mainly with fish, rice and other savoury dishes so that extra lemon juice can be squeezed on to the food. Lemon slices can be cut into a variety of shapes and used as decoration for sweet dishes. They are also refreshing added to water or any fruit juice or cocktail, and are indispensable in certain alcoholic drinks.

Below: Serve candied lemon strips dipped in chocolate as after-dinner treats.

CANDIED LEMONS
The candied slices can be served with meats such as pork or duck, or used in desserts. Slices can be soaked in orange liqueur before adding to desserts. Candied lemon slices are also delicious when simply dipped in chocolate and eaten as a sweet.

BUYING AND STORING LEMONS
• Always buy the largest and freshest lemons you can find.
• Choose fruit that is truly lemon yellow. Butter-yellow lemons may have lost some of their acidity in ripening.
• If possible buy unwaxed fruit, especially if you intend to use the skin.
• Whole lemons will keep fresh if kept in a cool place for approximately two weeks.
• Cut lemons should be wrapped in clear film (plastic wrap) and used as soon as possible.

Whole lemons

Lemon slices

Lemon wedges

Candied lemon slices

Candied lemon peel

Grated lemon rind

Lemon julienne

Lemon rind

LEMON TECHNIQUES AND SIMPLE RECIPES

If you intend to use the rind or peel of lemon in cooking, use a washed, unwaxed fruit.

ZESTING AND GRATING

1 To zest lemon, hold the fruit firmly in one hand. Scrape a lemon zester down the fruit.

2 If you need the zest to be even finer, brush it into a neat pile, hold a large chef's knife at right angles to the board and rock it back and forth.

3 To grate a lemon, hold it against the fine side of the grater and work it up and down, taking off only the zest and not the pith. Work over a small bowl to catch the rind.

JULIENNE STRIPS

1 Using a swivel-bladed vegetable peeler, remove the rind from washed unwaxed lemons in long, even strips. Slice into fine, long strips.

CITRUS CORKSCREWS

1 Using a cannelle knife (zester), pare long strips of rind from a washed, unwaxed lemon. The strips should be as long as it is possible to make them.

2 Pick up a cocktail stick (toothpick) and wind the strip of rind tightly around it. Slide the cocktail stick out to leave a little citrus corkscrew to hang over the edge of glasses or iced dessert dishes.

FRESH LEMON CURD

This classic tangy preserve is still one of the most popular of all the curds.

Makes about 450g/1lb

Grate 3 unwaxed lemons and squeeze the juice. Add to a pan with 115g/4oz/½ cup caster (superfine) sugar and stir over a low heat to dissolve the sugar. Mix 15ml/1 tbsp cornflour (cornstarch) with 15ml/1 tbsp water to make a paste and stir into the sugar syrup.

Remove from the heat and whisk in 2 egg yolks. Return to a low heat, whisk for about 2 minutes and remove from the heat. Gradually whisk in the butter. Pour into a sterilized jar, cover and seal at once. Leave to cool completely, then store in the refrigerator and use within three weeks.

LEMON AND PAPAYA RELISH

This chunky relish is best made with a firm, unripe papaya. It is excellent served with roast meats or with a robust cheese and crackers.

Makes about 450g/1lb

Peel a large unripe papaya and cut it lengthways in half. Remove the seeds with a small teaspoon. Cut the flesh into small chunks and place them in a large pan.

Thinly slice one onion and add the slices plus 40g/1½ oz/⅓ cup raisins to the papaya chunks, then stir in 250ml/8fl oz/1 cup red wine vinegar. Bring to the boil, lower the heat and simmer for approximately 10 minutes.

Add the juice of 2 lemons, 150ml/¼ pint/⅔ cup elderflower cordial, 165g/5½ oz/¾ cup sugar, 1 cinnamon stick and 1 fresh bay leaf to the pan and bring to the boil, stirring all the time.

Check that all the sugar has dissolved, then lower the heat and simmer for 50–60 minutes or until the relish thickens.

Ladle into hot sterilized jars. Seal and label and store for one week before using to allow the flavours to fully develop. Store in a cool place and keep chilled once opened. It will keep for up to four weeks.

To serve, rinse the preserved lemons to remove the salt, pull off the flesh and discard. Cut into strips and use as desired.

MAYONNAISE
Quick and easy to make, this classic sauce is often served with fish and chicken, in sandwiches and hamburgers.

CANDIED LEMON SLICES
Use these to decorate lemon tarts, ices and sorbets. They will keep for up to a week chilled.

Wash two large unwaxed lemons and cut into thin slices, put them in a pan and cover with plenty of water. Simmer for 15–20 minutes, then drain.

Put 200g/7oz/1 cup caster (superfine) sugar in a large, shallow pan and stir in 105ml/ 7 tbsp water. Heat to dissolve the sugar, stirring constantly, then bring to the boil. Boil for 2 minutes, add the lemon slices and cook for 15 minutes, until they look shiny and candied.

PRESERVED LEMONS
These are widely used in Middle Eastern cooking

Makes two 1.6 litre/2 pint jars
Wash 10 unwaxed lemons and cut each into eight wedges. Press a generous amount of salt into the wedges, pushing it into every crevice.

Pack the wedges into two 1.6 litre/2 pint sterilized jars. To each jar, add 30–45ml/ 2–3 tbsp salt and 90ml/6 tbsp lemon juice, then top up with boiing water, to cover the lemons. Cover the jars and leave to stand for two to four weeks before serving.

Makes 250ml/8fl oz/1 cup
Mix the egg yolk, 5ml/1 tsp mustard powder, 15ml/1 tbsp lemon juice in a bowl and season. Place the bowl on a wet kitchen towel to prevent it from moving while whisking. Pour 200ml/7fl ox/1 cup vegetable oil in a jug or pitcher.

Whisk the mixture vigorously while adding the oil drop by drop. When the sauce begins to thicken, the oil can be added a little more quickly, in a thin and steady stream until the sauce is thick and creamy. It may not be necessary to add all the oil.

HOLLANDAISE
This rich creamy lemon sauce is a standard accompaniment. Make it just before serving on Eggs Benedict, meat or fish.

Makes 135ml/4fl oz/½ cup
Melt 115g/4oz/½ cup unsalted (sweet) butter in a small pan. Put the 2 egg yolks and 30ml/ 2 tbsp lemon juice in a bowl.

Season and whisk until smooth. Pour the melted butter in a steady stream on to the egg yolk mixture, beating vigorously with a wooden spoon to make a smooth, creamy sauce.

LEMONADE
This traditional drink is perfect for a hot summer's day.

Makes 4 tall glasses
Pare the skin from 3 lemons and squeeze out the juice. Put the lemon rind and 115g/ 4oz/½ cup sugar into a bowl, add 900ml/1½ pints/3¾ cups boiling water and stir well until the sugar has dissolved. Cover and leave until cold.

Add the lemon juice, mix well and strain into a jug or pitcher. Chill and serve with plenty of ice.

LEMON VODKA
Similar to the Italian liqueur, Limoncello, this lemon vodka should be drunk sparingly.

Makes 12–15 shot glasses
Squeeze the juice from 10 large lemons and pour into a jug or pitcher. Add 275g/10oz/1¼ cup caster (superfine) sugar and whisk well until the sugar has dissolved. Strain the juice into a clean bottle and add 250ml/ 8fl oz/1 cup vodka. Shake well and chill for up to two weeks.

STARTERS, SALADS AND SIDE DISHES

THE LEMON'S FRAGRANT JUICE SHARPENS THE

FLAVOUR OF SOUPS AND SAVOURY SAUCES, ADDS

A CITRUS TANG TO SALADS AND PERFECTLY

BALANCES THE RICHNESS OF FRIED CHICKEN

AVGOLEMONO

This is a great favourite in Greece and is a fine example of how a few ingredients can make a marvellous dish if carefully chosen and cooked. It is essential to use a well-flavoured stock.

Serves 4

900ml/1½ pints/3¾ cups
   chicken stock, preferably
   home-made
50g/2oz/generous ⅓ cup long
   grain rice, rinsed and drained
3 egg yolks
30–60ml/2–4 tbsp lemon juice
30ml/2 tbsp finely chopped
   fresh parsley
salt and ground black pepper
lemon slices and parsley sprigs,
   to garnish

Energy 104kcal/438kJ; Protein 5.5g;
Carbohydrate 14.3g, of which sugars 0.7g;
Fat 3.2g, of which saturates 0.8g;
Cholesterol 95mg; Calcium 20mg;
Fibre 0.6g; Sodium 117mg.

Pour the stock into a pan, bring to simmering point, then add the drained rice. Half cover and cook for about 15 minutes or until the rice is just tender. Season with salt and pepper.

Whisk the egg yolks in a bowl, then add about 30ml/2 tbsp of the lemon juice, whisking constantly until the mixture is smooth and bubbly. Add a ladleful of soup and whisk again.

Remove the soup from the heat and slowly add the egg mixture, whisking all the time. The soup will turn a pretty lemon colour and will thicken slightly.

Taste and add more lemon juice if necessary. Stir in the chopped parsley. Serve at once, without reheating, garnished with lemon slices and parsley sprigs.

LEMON AND PUMPKIN MOULES MARINIÈRE

Based on the classic French shellfish dish, this mussel soup is thickened and flavoured with fresh pumpkin. The lemon counterbalances the rich oiliness of the shellfish.

Serves 4

1kg/2¼lb fresh mussels
300ml/½ pint/1¼ cups dry
  white wine
1 large lemon
1 bay leaf
15ml/1 tbsp olive oil
1 onion, chopped
1 garlic clove, crushed
675g/1½lb pumpkin or squash,
  seeded, peeled and roughly
  chopped
900ml/1½ pints/3¾ cups
  vegetable stock
30ml/2 tbsp chopped fresh dill
salt and ground black pepper
lemon wedges, to serve

Energy 126kcal/532kJ; Protein 13g;
Carbohydrate 7.5g, of which sugars 4g;
Fat 5g, of which saturates 0.8g;
Cholesterol 40mg; Calcium 113mg;
Fibre 2.5g; Sodium 245mg

Scrub the mussels in cold water and pull away the dark hairy beards protruding from the shells. Discard any open mussels that do not shut when tapped sharply, and put the rest into a large saucepan. Pour in the white wine.

Pare large pieces of rind from the lemon and squeeze the juice, then add both to the mussels with the bay leaf. Cover and bring to the boil, then cook for 4–5 minutes, shaking the pan occasionally until all the mussels have opened. Drain the mussels in a colander over a large bowl. Reserve the cooking liquid and the mussels.

Discard the lemon rind and bay leaf, and any mussels that have still not opened.

When all the mussels are cool enough to handle, set aside a few in their shells for the garnish. Remove the remaining mussels from their shells. Strain the reserved cooking liquid through a muslin-lined sieve to remove any sand or grit.

Heat the oil in a large, clean saucepan. Add the onion and garlic and cook for 4–5 minutes, until softened. Add the pumpkin flesh and the strained mussel cooking liquid. Bring to the boil and simmer, uncovered, for 5–6 minutes. Pour in the vegetable stock and cook for a further 25–30 minutes, until the pumpkin has almost disintegrated.

Cool the soup slightly, then process it in a food processor or blender until smooth. Return the soup to the rinsed-out saucepan and season well. Stir in the chopped dill and the shelled mussels, then bring just to the boil.

Ladle the soup into warmed soup plates and garnish with the reserved mussels in their shells. Serve lemon wedges with the soup.

LEMON AND SESAME CHICKEN

These delicate strips of chicken are at their best if you have time to leave them to marinate. The subtle fragrance of lemon really enhances the rich taste of fried chicken and the nutty sesame seeds.

Serves 4

4 large chicken breast fillets,
  skinned and cut into strips
15ml/1 tbsp light soy sauce
15ml/1 tbsp Chinese rice wine
2 garlic cloves, crushed
10ml/2 tsp finely grated fresh
  root ginger
1 egg, lightly beaten
150g/5oz cornflour (cornstarch)
sunflower oil, for frying
toasted sesame seeds, to sprinkle

For the sauce

15ml/1 tbsp sunflower oil
2 spring onions (scallions),
  finely sliced
1 garlic clove, crushed
10ml/2 tsp cornflour (cornstarch)
90ml/6 tbsp chicken stock
10ml/2 tsp finely grated lemon
  zest
30ml/2 tbsp lemon juice
10ml/2 tsp sugar
2.5ml/½ tsp sesame oil
salt

Place the chicken strips in a large, non-metallic bowl. Mix together the light soy sauce, rice wine, garlic and ginger and pour over the chicken. Toss together to combine.

Cover the chicken and place in the refrigerator for 8–10 hours, or overnight if time permits.

When ready to cook, add the beaten egg to the chicken and mix well, then tip the mixture into a colander to drain off any excess marinade and egg.

Place the cornflour in a large plastic bag and add the chicken pieces. Shake it vigorously to thoroughly coat the chicken strips.

Fill a wok one-third full of sunflower oil and heat to 180°C/350°F (or until a cube of bread, dropped into the oil, browns in 15 seconds).

Deep-fry the chicken, in batches, for 3–4 minutes. Lift out the chicken using a slotted spoon and drain on kitchen paper. Reheat the oil and deep-fry the chicken once more, in batches, for 2–3 minutes. Remove with a slotted spoon and drain on kitchen paper. Pour the oil out and wipe out the wok with kitchen paper.

To make the sauce, place the sunflower oil in a wok and heat. Add the spring onions and garlic and stir-fry for 1–2 minutes. Mix together the cornflour, stock, lemon zest, lemon juice, sugar, sesame oil and salt and pour into the wok. Cook over a high heat for 2–3 minutes until thickened. Return the chicken to the sauce, toss lightly and sprinkle over the toasted sesame seeds.

Energy 450kcal/1891kJ; Protein 38.2g; Carbohydrate 37.1g, of which sugars 2.5g; Fat 17.6g, of which saturates 2.6g; Cholesterol 157mg; Calcium 25mg; Fibre 0.1g; Sodium 396mg.

CAULIFLOWER WITH EGG AND LEMON

Cauliflower is completely delicious if cooked in the right way. Here it is teamed with a lemon sauce.
Try serving it with something rich, such as fried meatballs.

Serves 6

75–90ml/5–6 tbsp extra virgin
    olive oil
1 medium cauliflower, divided
    into large florets
2 eggs
juice of 1 lemon
5ml/1 tsp cornflour
    (cornstarch), mixed to a
    cream with a little cold water
30ml/2 tbsp chopped fresh flat
    leaf parsley
salt

Heat the olive oil in a large heavy pan, add the cauliflower florets and
sauté over a medium heat until they start to brown.

Pour in enough hot water to almost cover the cauliflower, add salt
to taste, then cover the pan and cook for 7–8 minutes until the florets
are just soft. Remove the pan from the heat and leave to stand, covered,
while you make the sauce.

Beat the eggs in a bowl, add the lemon juice and cornflour and beat
until well mixed. While beating, add a few tablespoons of the hot liquid
from the cauliflower. Pour the egg mixture slowly over the cauliflower,
then stir gently. Place the pan over a very low heat for 2 minutes to
thicken the sauce. Spoon into a warmed serving bowl, sprinkle the
chopped parsley over the top and serve.

Energy 201kcal/833kJ; Protein 7g; Carbohydrate 4.4g, of which sugars 2.7g; Fat 17.5g, of
which saturates 3g; Cholesterol 95mg; Calcium 51mg; Fibre 2.2g; Sodium 47mg.

ARTICHOKES WITH GARLIC, LEMON AND OLIVE OIL

This classic Italian dish is said to be of Jewish origin. It is not only wonderful as a salad, but can also be added to roasted fish, chicken or lamb during cooking.

Serves 4

4 globe artichokes
juice of 1–2 lemons, plus extra to acidulate water
60ml/4 tbsp extra virgin olive oil
1 onion, chopped
5–8 garlic cloves, roughly chopped or thinly sliced
30ml/2 tbsp chopped fresh parsley, plus extra to garnish
120ml/4fl oz/½ cup dry white wine
120ml/4fl oz/½ cup vegetable stock or water
salt and ground black pepper

COOK'S TIP
Placing trimmed artichokes in a bowl of acidulated water prevents them from discolouring.

Energy 142kcal/586kJ; Protein 1.6g;
Carbohydrate 4.1g, of which sugars 1.9g;
Fat 11.3g, of which saturates 1.6g;
Cholesterol 0mg; Calcium 40mg;
Fibre 1.6g; Sodium 47mg.

Prepare the artichokes. Pull back and snap off the tough leaves. Peel the tender part of the stems and cut into bitesize pieces, then put in a bowl of acidulated water. Cut the artichokes into quarters and cut out the inside thistle heart. Add them to the bowl.

Heat the oil in a pan, add the onion and garlic and fry for 5 minutes until softened. Stir in the parsley and cook for a few seconds. Add the wine, stock and drained artichokes. Season with half the lemon juice, salt and pepper.

Bring the mixture to the boil, then lower the heat, cover and simmer for 10–15 minutes until the artichokes are tender. Lift the artichokes out with a slotted spoon and transfer to a serving dish.

Bring the cooking liquid to the boil and boil until reduced to about half its volume. Pour the mixture over the artichokes, drizzle over the remaining lemon juice and sprinkle with parsley. Cool before serving.

LEMONY COUSCOUS SALAD

There are many ways of serving couscous and this fragrant salad is popular almost everywhere.
It has a delicate flavour and is excellent with grilled chicken or kebabs.

Serves 4

275g/10oz/1²/₃ cups couscous
525ml/18fl oz/2¹/₄ cups boiling
vegetable stock
16–20 black olives
2 small courgettes (zucchini)
25g/1oz/¹/₄ cup flaked almonds,
toasted
60ml/4 tbsp olive oil
15ml/1 tbsp lemon juice
15ml/1 tbsp chopped fresh
coriander (cilantro)
15ml/1 tbsp chopped fresh
parsley
good pinch of ground cumin
good pinch of cayenne pepper
salt

Energy 123kcal/509kJ; Protein 1g;
Carbohydrate 4g, of which sugars 4g;
Fat 12g, of which saturates 2g;
Cholesterol 0mg; Calcium 44mg; Fibre 1g;
Sodium 176mg.

Place the couscous in a bowl and pour over the boiling stock. Stir with a fork and then set aside for 10 minutes for the stock to be absorbed. Fluff up with a fork.

Halve the olives, discarding the stones. Top and tail the courgettes and cut into small julienne strips. Carefully mix the courgettes, olives and almonds into the couscous.

Blend together the olive oil, lemon juice, herbs, spices and a pinch of salt, and stir into the salad.

MAIN MEALS

WHETHER ADDED TO MARINADES, SAUCES,
BATTERS OR SAVOURY BUTTERS, OR SIMPLY
SPRINKLED OVER GRILLED FISH, LEMON JUICE
LENDS A PIQUANT AND FLAVOUR-ENHANCING
FRESHNESS. LEMON ALSO COMBINES BEAUTIFULLY
WITH POULTRY AND CUTS THE RICHNESS OF RED
MEATS SUCH AS LAMB.

FRIED SARDINES WITH LEMON

This simple street dish is generally made with small sardines or sprats. They are best served gutted and are particularly delicious when steeped in lemon juice before frying.

Serves 4

450g/1lb fresh small sardines, gutted and cleaned
300ml/½ pint/1¼ cups lemon juice
60–75ml/4–5 tbsp chickpea or plain (all-purpose) flour
olive or sunflower oil for deep frying
salt and ground black pepper
2 lemons, halved, to serve

First marinate the fish. Place the sardines in a large shallow dish and pour the lemon juice over them. Cover and chill for 1–2 hours, then drain and pat dry.

Rub the fish with a little salt and pepper and dip them in the flour until lightly coated. Heat enough oil for deep-frying in a heavy pan.

Fry the fish in batches for 5–6 minutes, until crisp and golden. Drain them on kitchen paper and serve while still hot, with lemon halves to squeeze over them.

Energy 358kcal/1488kJ; Protein 18.7g;
Carbohydrate 11.7g, of which sugars 0.2g;
Fat 26.5g, of which saturates 4.4g;
Cholesterol 0mg; Calcium 107mg;
Fibre 0.5g; Sodium 96mg

SEA BASS BAKED IN A PARCEL WITH LEMON AND HERBS

This is a simple way of keeping a whole fish moist in a foil parcel. Use smaller fish for individual parcels, one for each guest if you wish. You can also use salmon or red mullet for this recipe.

Serves 4

1 x 2kg/4½lb whole sea bass, cleaned and descaled
1 lemon, thinly sliced
3 sprigs fresh rosemary
3 fresh bay leaves
2 garlic cloves, peeled and quartered
4 spring onions (scallions), chopped
45ml/3 tbsp olive oil
salt and ground black pepper
fresh bread, to serve

Preheat the oven to 200°C/400°F/Gas 6.

Cut two large pieces of foil, each about 60 x 60cm/24 x 24 in, and put them on top of each other. Put the fish in the middle of the sheets of foil and put the lemon, rosemary, bay leaves, garlic and spring onions inside and around the fish.

Turn up the ends of the foil and pour the oil over the fish. Season with salt and pepper. Crimp the foil edges together to make a parcel, leaving space for some air around the fish.

Place the parcel on a metal tray. Bake the sea bass in the oven for 30 minutes. Carefully take out the foil parcel, and place it on a warmed serving plate.

Take the parcel to the table and open it in front of your guests so they all enjoy the aroma. Carefully lift fillets of fish from the bone, and serve with some of the filling and some fresh bread.

Energy 487kcal/2039kJ; Protein 73g; Carbohydrate 2g, of which sugars 2g; Fat 21g, of which saturates 3g; Cholesterol 300mg; Calcium 520mg; Fibre 0.6g; Sodium 360mg.

HAKE WITH SPINACH AND EGG AND LEMON SAUCE

This simple, quick, delicious and healthy dish is a particular favourite in the Mediterranean. Be sure to wash the spinach thoroughly to get rid of any grit.

Serves 4

500g/1¼lb fresh spinach, trimmed of thick stalks
4 x 200g/7oz fresh hake steaks or 4 pieces of cod fillet
30ml/2 tbsp plain (all-purpose) flour
75ml/5 tbsp extra virgin olive oil
1 glass white wine (175ml/6fl oz/¾ cup)
3–4 strips of pared lemon rind
salt and ground black pepper

For the egg and lemon sauce

2 large (US extra large) eggs at room temperature
juice of ½ lemon
2.5ml/½ tsp cornflour (cornstarch)

Place the spinach leaves in a large pan with just the water that clings to the leaves after washing. Cover the pan tightly and cook over a medium heat for 5–7 minutes, until they are cooked. Remove the lid occasionally and turn the leaves using a wooden spoon. Drain and set the spinach aside.

Dust the fish lightly with the flour and shake off any excess. Heat the olive oil in a large frying pan, add the pieces of fish and sauté gently, for 2–3 minutes on each side, until the flesh starts to turn golden.

Pour the wine over the fish, add the lemon rind and some seasoning and carefully shake the pan from side to side to blend the flavourings. Lower the heat and simmer gently for a few minutes until the wine has reduced a little.

Add the spinach, distributing it evenly around the fish. Let it simmer for 3–4 minutes more, then pull the pan off the heat and let it stand for a few minutes before adding the sauce.

To prepare the egg and lemon sauce, whisk together the eggs, lemon juice and cornflour over a gentle heat. Pour the sauce over the fish and spinach, place the pan over a very gentle heat and shake to amalgamate the ingredients. If it appears too dry add a little warm water. Allow to cook gently for 2–3 minutes and serve.

Energy 490kcal/2041kJ; Protein 45g;
Carbohydrate 9g, of which sugars 2g;
Fat 28g, of which saturates 4g; Cholesterol
173mg; Calcium 275mg; Fibre 5g;
Sodium 424mg.

GRILLED SOLE WITH CHIVE AND LEMON GRASS BUTTER

Chives are at their best when barely cooked, and they make a delicious butter when teamed with lemon grass to serve with simple grilled fish. Halibut, turbot and swordfish would also work well.

Serves 4

115g/4oz/½ cup unsalted butter, softened, plus extra melted butter
5ml/1 tsp minced lemon grass
pinch of finely grated lemon rind
45ml/3 tbsp snipped chives or chopped chive flowers, plus extra chives or chive flowers to garnish
2.5–5ml/½–1 tsp Thai fish sauce
4 sole, skinned
salt and ground black pepper
steamed new potatoes, finely sliced cumumber and lemon wedges, to serve

Energy 254kcal/1066kJ; Protein 21.5g;
Carbohydrate 25.6g, of which sugars 0.8g;
Fat 7.9g, of which saturates 0.7g;
Cholesterol 50mg; Calcium 100mg;
Fibre 1.6g; Sodium 105mg.

Cream the butter with the lemon grass, lemon rind, and chives or chive flowers. Season to taste with Thai fish sauce, salt and pepper.

Chill the butter mixture to firm it for a short while, then form it into a roll and wrap in foil, clear film (plastic wrap) or greaseproof paper. Chill until firm. Preheat the grill (broiler).

Brush the fish with a little melted butter. Place it on the grill rack and season. Grill (broil) for about 5 minutes on each side, until firm and just cooked. Meanwhile, cut the chilled butter into thin slices. Serve the fish topped with slices of the butter.

Serve immediately, with steamed new potatoes and finely sliced cucumber, garnished with chives. Offer lemon wedges with the fish.

HOT SPICY PRAWNS WITH LEMON AND CORIANDER

This is a quick and easy way of preparing prawns for an appetizing mid-week supper. Serve the prawns with plenty of bread to mop up the tasty juices.

Serves 4

120ml/8 tbsp olive oil
5 garlic cloves, chopped
50g/2oz fresh root ginger,
    peeled and shredded
2 chillies, seeded and chopped
10ml/2 tsp cumin seed
juice of 2 lemons
10ml/2 tsp paprika
900g/2lb uncooked king prawns
    (jumbo shrimp), shelled
bunch of fresh coriander
    (cilantro), chopped
salt
2 lemons, cut into wedges and
    fresh bread, to serve

Energy 382kcal/1591kJ; Protein 40.8g;
Carbohydrate 1.1g, of which sugars 0.9g;
Fat 23.9g, of which saturates 3.4g;
Cholesterol 439mg; Calcium 254mg;
Fibre 1.9g; Sodium 440mg

In a large, heavy frying pan, heat the oil with the garlic.

Stir in the ginger, chilli, cumin seeds and lemon juice. Cook briefly, until the ingredients give off a lovely aroma, then add the paprika and toss in the prawns.

Fry the prawns over a fairly high heat, turning them frequently, for 3–5 minutes, until just cooked. Season to taste with salt and add the fresh coriander. Serve immediately, with lemon wedges for squeezing over the prawns and fresh bread.

BAKED LEMON PLAICE

Plaice is a delicately flavoured fish that is best cooked in a simple fish stock. The addition of crushed dry biscuit gives extra texture to this dish and the lemon slices lift the flavours beautifully.

Serves 4

2 plaice or flounder, 1kg/2¼lb
1 carrot, chopped
1 leek, chopped
1 stick celery, chopped
1 bay leaf
5ml/1 tsp parsley, chopped
50g/2oz/¼ cup butter, plus
    extra for greasing
juice of 1 lemon
freshly grated nutmeg
4 thin lemon slices
4 coarsely cut sage leaves
4 plain dry biscuits (cookies),
    crushed
chives, to garnish
salt and ground black pepper

Cut off the tail and head from the fish with a sharp knife and snip off the fins with kitchen scissors. Remove and discard the gills. Put the fish trimmings and the chopped carrot, leek and celery with the bay leaf and parsley in a large pan, season and add water to cover. Bring to the boil, then lower the heat, cover and simmer for 1 hour. Strain the stock into a bowl and leave to cool.

Preheat the oven to 200°C/400°F/Gas 6. Grease an ovenproof dish with butter. Cut the fish into six thick strips and push out the guts. Add the lemon juice to a bowl of water, rinse the fish strips, and pat dry with kitchen paper.

Sprinkle the fish strips with nutmeg and season with salt and pepper.

Place the strips upright, with the cut sides underneath them, in the prepared dish and tuck the lemon slices in between.

Measure 200ml/7fl oz/scant 1 cup of the fish stock and pour it around the fish.

Sprinkle with the sage and cover with the crushed biscuits. Dot the butter over the top and bake for 20 minutes. Garnish the fish with chopped chives, and serve hot.

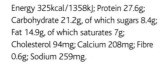

Energy 325kcal/1358kJ; Protein 27.6g;
Carbohydrate 21.2g, of which sugars 8.4g;
Fat 14.9g, of which saturates 7g;
Cholesterol 94mg; Calcium 208mg; Fibre
0.6g; Sodium 259mg.

VERMICELLI WITH LEMON

Fresh and tangy, this makes an excellent quick and easy midweek supper dish. It doesn't rely on fresh seasonal ingredients, so it is good at any time of year.

Serves 4

350g/12oz dried vermicelli
juice of 2 large lemons, plus thin julienne strips, to garnish
50g/2oz/¼ cup butter
200ml/7fl oz/scant 1 cup panna da cucina or double (heavy) cream
115g/4oz/1⅓ cups freshly grated Parmesan cheese
salt and ground black pepper

COOK'S TIP
Lemons vary in the amount of juice they yield. On average, a large fresh lemon will yield 60–90ml/4–6 tbsp. The lemony flavour of this dish is quite sharp so use less juice, if you prefer.

Cook the pasta in salted boiling water according to the instructions on the packet.

Meanwhile, pour the lemon juice into a medium pan. Add the butter and cream, then salt and pepper to taste.

Bring to the boil, then lower the heat and simmer for about 5 minutes, stirring occasionally, until the cream reduces slightly.

Drain the pasta and return it to the pan. Add the grated Parmesan, then taste the sauce for seasoning and pour it over the pasta. Toss quickly over a medium heat until the pasta is evenly coated with the sauce, then serve immediately, garnished with lemon julienne.

Energy 706kcal/2934kJ; Protein 20.3g; Carbohydrate 70.4g, of which sugars 1.9g; Fat 37.9g, of which saturates 24.6g; Cholesterol 61mg; Calcium 406mg; Fibre 0.1g; Sodium 420mg.

LEEK, MUSHROOM AND LEMON RISOTTO

Leeks and lemon go together beautifully in this light risotto, while mushrooms add texture and extra flavour. It is true comfort food for any time of year.

Serves 4

225g/8oz trimmed leeks
225g/8oz/2–3 cups brown cap
*   mushrooms*
30ml/2 tbsp olive oil
3 garlic cloves, crushed
75g/3oz/6 tbsp butter
1 large onion, roughly chopped
350g/12oz/1¾ cups risotto rice
1.2 litres/2 pints/5 cups
*   simmering vegetable stock*
grated rind of 1 lemon
45ml/3 tbsp lemon juice
50g/2oz/²⁄₃ cup freshly grated
*   Parmesan cheese*
60ml/4 tbsp mixed chopped
*   fresh chives and flat leaf*
*   parsley*
salt and ground black pepper

Slice the leeks in half lengthways, wash them well and then slice them evenly. Wipe the mushrooms with kitchen paper and chop them roughly.

Heat the oil in a large saucepan and cook the garlic for 1 minute. Add the leeks, mushrooms and plenty of seasoning and cook over a medium heat for about 10 minutes, or until the leeks have softened and browned. Spoon into a bowl and set aside.

Add 25g/1oz/2 tbsp of the butter to the pan. As soon as it has melted, add the onion and cook over a medium heat for 5 minutes until it has softened and is golden.

Stir in the rice and cook for about 1 minute until the grains begin to look translucent and are coated in the fat. Add a ladleful of stock and cook gently, stirring occasionally, until the liquid has been absorbed.

Continue to add stock, a ladleful at a time, until all of it has been absorbed, stirring constantly. This should take about 25–30 minutes. The risotto will turn thick and creamy and the rice should be tender but not sticky.

Just before serving, add the leeks and mushrooms, with the remaining butter. Stir in the grated lemon rind and juice. Add the grated Parmesan cheese and the herbs. Adjust the seasoning and serve immediately.

Energy 442kcal/1844kJ; Protein 11.8g;
Carbohydrate 77.6g, of which sugars 5.6g;
Fat 9g, of which saturates 3.8g;
Cholesterol 14mg; Calcium 128mg;
Fibre 2.9g; Sodium 97mg

TAGINE OF SPICED MEATBALLS WITH LEMON AND SPICES

The meatballs in this aromatic Moroccan dish are poached gently with lemon and spices to make a meal that is quite light and ideal for lunch. Serve it with a salad or plain couscous.

Serves 4

450g/1lb finely minced (ground) lamb
3 large onions, grated
small bunch of flat leaf parsley, chopped
5–10ml/1–2 tsp ground cinnamon
5ml/1 tsp ground cumin
pinch of cayenne pepper
40g/1½oz/3 tbsp butter
25g/1oz fresh root ginger, peeled and finely chopped
1 hot chilli, seeded and finely chopped
pinch of saffron threads
small bunch of fresh coriander (cilantro), finely chopped
juice of 1 lemon
300ml/½ pint/1¼ cups water
1 lemon, quartered
salt and ground black pepper
crusty bread, to serve

To make the meatballs, pound the minced lamb in a bowl by using your hand to lift it up and slap it back down into the bowl.

Knead in half the grated onions, the parsley, cinnamon, cumin and cayenne pepper. Season with salt and pepper, and continue pounding the mixture by hand for a few minutes. Break off pieces of the mixture and shape them into walnut-size balls.

In a heavy lidded frying pan, melt the butter and add the remaining onion with the ginger, chilli and saffron. Stirring frequently, cook gently until the onion begins to colour, then stir in the chopped fresh coriander and lemon juice.

Pour in the water, season with salt and bring to the boil. Drop in the meatballs, reduce the heat and cover the pan. Poach the meatballs gently, turning them occasionally, for about 20 minutes.

Remove the lid, tuck the lemon quarters around the meatballs and cook, uncovered, for a further 10 minutes to reduce the liquid slightly. Serve hot, straight from the pan with lots of crusty fresh bread to mop up the delicious juices.

Energy 334kcal/1386kJ; Protein 18g; Carbohydrate 5g, of which sugars 4g; Fat 27g, of which saturates 6g; Cholesterol 57mg; Calcium 48mg; Fibre 2g; Sodium 190mg.

POT-ROASTED CHICKEN WITH PRESERVED LEMONS

Roasting chicken and potatoes in this way gives an interesting variety of textures. The chicken and potatoes on the top crisp up, while underneath they stay soft and juicy.

Serves 4–6

675g/1½lb potatoes, unpeeled
30ml/2 tbsp olive oil
6–8 pieces of preserved lemon
1.3kg/3lb corn-fed chicken,
*   jointed*
salt and ground black pepper
steamed carrots or curly kale, to
*   serve*

Preheat the oven to 190°C/375°F/Gas 5. Cut the potatoes into even-sized chunks.

Drizzle the olive oil into the bottom of a large roasting pan. Spread the chunks of potato in a single layer in the pan and tuck in the pieces of preserved lemon.

Pour about 1cm/½in of cold water into the roasting pan. Arrange the chicken pieces on top and season with plenty of salt and black pepper. Roast for 45 minutes–1 hour, or until the chicken is cooked through, and serve with steamed green vegetables.

Energy 536kcal/2233kJ; Protein 28.3g; Carbohydrate 26.8g, of which sugars 2.2g; Fat 35.7g, of which saturates 8.4g; Cholesterol 133mg; Calcium 21mg; Fibre 1.7g; Sodium 123mg.

KLEFTIKO

This delicious Greek recipe for slow-cooked leg of lamb with potatoes, lemon and oregano is perfect to serve for Sunday lunch, and is not at all complicated.

Serves 6
45ml/3 tbsp olive oil
30ml/2 tbsp chopped fresh oregano or marjoram
30ml/2 tbsp fresh thyme, chopped
1 leg of lamb – about 2.5kg/5½lb
1 whole bulb of garlic, unpeeled and sliced in two through the equator
600g/1lb 6oz small waxy potatoes, washed
2 lemons, quartered
3 fresh bay leaves
200ml/7fl oz/scant 1 cup dry white wine
salt and ground black pepper
flat bread, and spinach salad, to serve

Preheat the oven to 180°C/350°F/Gas 4. Mix together the oil, oregano and thyme and then use your hands to rub it all over the lamb. Place the lamb in a large ovenproof dish that has a close-fitting lid.

Place the halved garlic bulb, potatoes, lemon quarters and bay leaves around the lamb, then pour the wine into the bottom of the dish. Season well with salt and pepper.

Put some foil over the dish and place the lid on top – this gives a very tight seal around the lid, which will keep the meat moist.

Place the ovenproof dish in the middle of the oven and leave the lamb to cook for 3–4 hours, until it is meltingly tender and falling off the bone; the potatoes will now be completely tender.

Once the lamb is cooked, take the ovenproof dish out of the oven. Serve the meat in chunks pulled from the bone, as it will be too tender to slice, with torn flatbread and a salad of baby spinach.

Energy 400kcal/1671kJ; Protein 36g; Carbohydrate 17g, of which sugars 2g; Fat 21g, of which saturates 7g; Cholesterol 123mg; Calcium 37mg; Fibre 1.3g; Sodium 194mg.

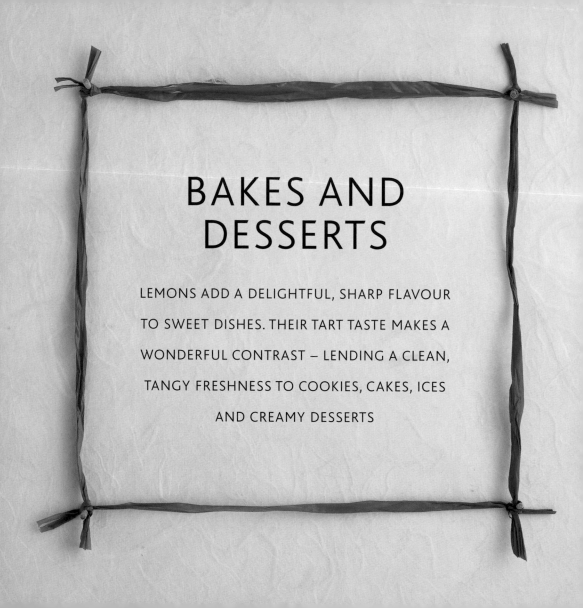

BAKES AND DESSERTS

LEMONS ADD A DELIGHTFUL, SHARP FLAVOUR
TO SWEET DISHES. THEIR TART TASTE MAKES A
WONDERFUL CONTRAST – LENDING A CLEAN,
TANGY FRESHNESS TO COOKIES, CAKES, ICES
AND CREAMY DESSERTS

LUSCIOUS LEMON BARS

A crisp cookie base is covered with a tangy lemon topping. The bars make an appealing addition to the tea table on a warm summer's day in the garden.

Makes 12

*150g/5oz/1¼ cups plain
   (all-purpose) flour
90g/3½oz/7 tbsp unsalted
   (sweet) butter, chilled and
   diced
50g/2oz/½ cup icing
   (confectioners') sugar, sifted*

For the topping

*2 eggs
175g/6oz/scant 1 cup caster
   (superfine) sugar
finely grated rind and juice of
   1 large lemon
15ml/1 tbsp plain (all-purpose)
   flour
2.5ml/½ tsp bicarbonate of
   soda (baking soda)
icing (confectioners') sugar, for
   dusting*

Energy 189kcal/795kJ; Protein 2.5g;
Carbohydrate 30.3g, of which sugars 19.8g;
Fat 7.3g, of which saturates 4.2g;
Cholesterol 48mg; Calcium 35mg;
Fibre 0.4g; Sodium 59mg.

Preheat the oven to 180°C/350°F/Gas 4. Line the base of a 20cm/ 8 in square shallow cake tin (pan) with baking parchment and lightly grease the sides of the tin.

Process the flour, butter and icing sugar in a food processor until the mixture comes together as a firm dough. Press evenly into the base of the tin and spread smoothly using the back of a tablespoon. Bake for 12–15 minutes until lightly golden. Cool in the tin.

To make the topping, whisk the eggs in a bowl until frothy. Add the caster sugar, a little at a time, whisking well between each addition. Whisk in the lemon rind and juice, flour and soda. Pour over the cookie base. Bake for 20–25 minutes, until set and golden.

Allow to cool slightly. Cut into twelve bars and dust with icing sugar. Leave to cool completely.

LEMON AND POPPY SEED MUFFINS

The addition of poppy seeds adds an unexpectedly light and crunchy texture to the cake crumb, which traditionally is soaked in a sweet lemon syrup.

Makes 8 tall muffins

225g/8oz/2 cups self-raising
   (self-rising) flour
200g/7oz/1 cup caster
   (superfine) sugar
40g/1½oz ground almonds
2 eggs, beaten
75g/3oz/6 tbsp unsalted
   (sweet) butter, melted
50ml/2fl oz/¼ cup vegetable oil
25ml/1½ tbsp poppy seeds
30ml/2 tbsp lemon juice
grated rind of 1 lemon
grated rind of 1 clementine

For the syrup

115g/4oz/generous ½ cup
   caster (superfine) sugar
50ml/2fl oz/¼ cup lemon juice
15ml/1 tbsp elderflower cordial
lemon segments, to decorate

Preheat the oven to 180°C/350°F/Gas 4. Grease and line 8 dariole moulds with baking parchment.

Sift the flour and sugar into a bowl. Stir in the ground almonds. Make a well in the centre.

In a jug or pitcher mix together the eggs, butter, oil, poppy seeds, lemon juice and the grated fruit rinds.

Pour the liquid into the flour mix and stir until just combined.

Fill the lined moulds three-quarters full and bake for 25 minutes. Leave to stand for a few minutes, then transfer to a wire rack to go completely cold.

To make the syrup, put the sugar, 120ml/4fl oz/½ cup water and the lemon juice in a pan and heat gently, stirring frequently until dissolved.

Leave to boil without stirring for 5–6 minutes until syrupy. Remove from the heat. Stir in the cordial.

Prick holes in the top of each muffin using a skewer. Pour over the warm syrup. Store for up to one week. Decorate the muffin tops with thin segments of lemon, before serving.

Energy 408kcal/1717kJ; Protein 5.9g;
Carbohydrate 63.9g, of which sugars 42.4g;
Fat 16.1g, of which saturates 6.2g;
Cholesterol 69mg; Calcium 94mg; Fibre
1.4g; Sodium 92mg.

VARIATION

For a breakfast treat, omit the syrup, break open the freshly baked muffin and spread it with butter and fresh lemon curd instead

LEMON DRIZZLE CAKE

Wonderfully moist and lemony, this cake is perfect for afternoon tea. A lemon and sugar syrup is poured over the cooked cake and allowed to soak through, so that the whole cake is sweet and tangy.

Serves 6–8

225g/8oz/1 cup unsalted (sweet) butter, softened, plus extra for greasing
finely grated rind of 2 lemons
175g/6oz/scant 1 cup, plus 5ml/1 tsp caster (superfine) sugar
4 eggs
225g/8oz/2 cups self-raising (self-rising) flour
5ml/1 tsp baking powder
shredded rind of 1 lemon, to decorate

For the syrup

juice of 1 lemon
150g/5oz/¾ cup caster (superfine) sugar

Energy 659kcal/2765kJ; Protein 8g; Carbohydrate 84.1g, of which sugars 56.2g; Fat 34.8g, of which saturates 21.4g; Cholesterol 213mg; Calcium 184mg; Fibre 1.2g; Sodium 466mg.

Preheat the oven to 160°C/325°F/Gas 3. Grease and line the base and sides of an 18–20cm/7–8 in round deep cake tin (pan) with baking parchment.

Mix the lemon rind and sugar together in a large bowl. Beat the butter with the lemon and sugar mixture until light and fluffy, then beat in the eggs one at a time.

Sift the flour and baking powder into the mixture in three batches and beat well.

Turn the batter into the prepared tin and smooth the top level. Bake for 1½ hours, or until golden brown and springy to the touch.

To make the syrup, slowly heat the juice with the sugar until dissolved.

Prick the cake top with a skewer and pour over the syrup. Sprinkle over the shredded lemon rind and 5ml/1 tsp sugar, then leave to cool. Remove the lining paper.

LEMON MERINGUE PIE

This popular dessert is a 20th-century development of older English cheesecakes – open tarts with a filling of curds. The pie is best served at room temperature, with or without cream.

Serves 6

For the pastry

115g/4oz/1 cup plain (all-purpose) flour
pinch of salt
25g/1oz/2 tbsp lard, diced
25g/1oz/2 tbsp butter, diced

For the filling

50g/2oz/¼ cup cornflour (cornstarch)
175g/6oz/¾ cup caster (superfine) sugar
finely grated rind and juice of 2 lemons
2 egg yolks
15g/½oz/1 tbsp butter, diced

For the meringue topping

2 egg whites
75g/3oz/½ cup caster (superfine) sugar

Energy 357kcal/1497kJ; Protein 6.8g;
Carbohydrate 42.8g, of which sugars 25.1g;
Fat 18.9g, of which saturates 9g;
Cholesterol 129mg; Calcium 108mg; Fibre
0.7g; Sodium 137mg

To make the pastry, sift the flour and salt into a bowl and add the lard and butter. With the fingertips, lightly rub the fats into the flour until the mixture resembles fine crumbs.

Stir in about 20ml/2 tbsp cold water until the mixture can be gathered together into a smooth ball of dough. Wrap the pastry and refrigerate for at least 30 minutes. Meanwhile, preheat the oven to 200°C/400°F/Gas 6.

Roll out the pastry on a lightly floured surface and use to line a 20cm/8 in flan tin (pan). Prick the base with a fork, line with baking parchment and add a layer of baking beans to prevent the pastry rising.

Put the pastry case (pie shell) into the hot oven and cook for 15 minutes. Remove the beans and parchment or foil, return the pastry to the oven and cook for a further 5 minutes until crisp and golden brown. Reduce the oven temperature to 150°C/300°F/Gas 2.

To make the lemon filling, put the cornflour into a pan and add the sugar, lemon rind and 300ml/½ pint/1¼ cups water. Heat the mixture, stirring continuously, until it comes to the boil and thickens. Reduce the heat and simmer very gently for 1 minute. Remove from the heat and stir in the lemon juice.

Add the the egg yolks to the lemon mixture, one at a time and beating after each addition, and then stir in the butter. Tip the mixture into the baked pastry case and level the surface.

To make the meringue topping, whisk the egg whites until stiff peaks form then whisk in half the sugar. Fold in the rest of the sugar using a metal spoon.

Spread the meringue over the lemon filling, covering it completely. Cook for about 20 minutes until lightly browned.

LEMON TART

This delightful tangy lemon tart uses lots of freshly grated lemon rind for a really intense flavour.
Serve it cold with a small glass of Limoncello for a delicious grown-up dessert.

Serves 6

250g/9oz/2¼ cups plain
    (all-purpose) flour, plus extra
    for dusting
125g/4¼oz/generous ½ cup
    cold unsalted (sweet) butter,
    chopped, plus softened butter
    for greasing
115g/4oz/½ cup caster
    (superfine) sugar
1 egg, plus 1 egg yolk
icing (confectioners') sugar,
    for dusting

For the filling

250ml/8fl oz/1 cup custard
115g/4oz/½ cup caster
    (superfine) sugar
finely grated rind of 3–4
    unwaxed lemons
250g/9oz/1 cup ricotta cheese
1 egg, beaten

Energy 605kcal/2539kJ; Protein 12.2g;
Carbohydrate 80.5g, of which sugars 46.7g;
Fat 28.3g, of which saturates 15.9g;
Cholesterol 162mg; Calcium 149mg; Fibre
1.3g; Sodium 218mg.

Put the plain flour in a bowl. Add the chopped butter and rub it in until the mixture resembles fine breadcrumbs.

Stir in the sugar and add the egg and egg yolk. Mix to a soft dough. Knead lightly, wrap in clear film (plastic wrap) and chill until required.

While the pastry is resting, make the filling. Heat the custard and stir in the sugar and lemon rind until the sugar is dissolved, then cover the surface of the custard with baking parchment and leave it to cool.

Preheat the oven to 180°C/350°F/Gas 4. Grease a 20cm/8 in tart tin (pan) with butter. Beat the ricotta into the custard, then add the beaten egg. Mix thoroughly.

On a large sheet of baking parchment, roll out the pastry using a lightly floured rolling pin. Line the tart tin and trim the edges.

Pour the lemon filling into the tart case and bake in the oven for 30 minutes. Leave to cool, then dust with icing sugar. Serve at room temperature or cold.

LEMON ROULADE WITH LEMON-CURD CREAM

This feather-light roulade is flavoured with almonds and filled with a rich lemon-curd cream. Use good-quality or home-made lemon curd for that perfect touch. Eat this cake fresh for the best taste.

Serves 8

butter, for greasing
4 eggs, separated
115g/4oz/generous ½ cup
*   caster (superfine) sugar*
finely grated rind of 2 lemons,
*   plus extra to decorate*
5ml/1 tsp vanilla extract
40g/1½oz/⅓ cup plain
*   (all-purpose) flour*
25g/1oz/¼ cup ground
*   almonds*

For the lemon-curd cream

300ml/½ pint/1¼ cups double
*   (heavy) cream*
60ml/4 tbsp lemon curd
45ml/3 tbsp icing
*   (confectioners') sugar, for*
*   dusting*

Preheat the oven to 190°C/375°F/Gas 5. Grease and line a 33 × 23cm/13 × 9in Swiss roll tin (jelly roll pan) with baking parchment.

In a large bowl, beat the egg yolks with half the sugar until foamy. Beat in the lemon rind and vanilla extract.

Sift the flour over the egg mixture and lightly fold in with the ground almonds, using a metal spoon.

Put the egg whites into a clean, grease-free bowl and whisk until they form stiff, glossy peaks. Gradually whisk in the remaining sugar to form a stiff meringue.

Stir half the meringue mixture into the egg yolk mixture to slacken it. When combined, fold in the remainder of the meringue mixture.

Pour the batter into the prepared tin and smooth level. Bake for 10 minutes, or until risen and spongy to the touch.

Put the tin on a wire rack and cover loosely with a sheet of baking parchment and a damp dish towel. Leave to cool.

To make the lemon curd-cream, whip the cream until it holds its shape, then fold in the lemon curd.

Sift the icing sugar over a piece of baking parchment. Turn the sponge out on to it. Peel off the lining paper and spread over the filling.

Using the paper, roll up the sponge from one long side. Sprinkle with lemon rind.

Energy 337kcal/1401kJ; Protein 5g; Carbohydrate 24.5g, of which sugars 18.9g; Fat 25.1g, of which saturates 13.6g; Cholesterol 148mg; Calcium 55mg; Fibre 0.4g; Sodium 50mg.

LEMON SORBET

This is probably the most classic sorbet of all. Refreshingly tangy and yet deliciously smooth, it quite literally melts in the mouth. It is the perfect choice for serving after a spicy main course.

Serves 6

200g/7oz/1 cup caster (superfine) sugar
300ml/½ pint/1¼ cups water
4 lemons, well scrubbed
1 egg white
sugared lemon rind, to decorate

COOK'S TIP

Cut one third off the top of a lemon and retain as a lid. Squeeze the juice out of the larger portion. Remove any membrane and use the shell as a ready-made container. Scoop or pipe sorbet into the shell, top with lid and add lemon leaves or small bay leaves. Serve one lemon per person on a bed of crushed ice.

Energy 134kcal/571kJ; Protein 0.7g;
Carbohydrate 35g, of which sugars 35g; Fat
0g, of which saturates 0g; Cholesterol 0mg;
Calcium 19mg; Fibre 0g; Sodium 12mg.

Put the sugar and water into a saucepan and bring to the boil, stirring occasionally until the sugar has just dissolved.

Using a swivel vegetable peeler, pare the rind thinly from two of the lemons so that it falls straight into the pan.

Simmer for 2 minutes without stirring, then take the pan off the heat. Leave to cool, then chill.

Squeeze the juice from all the lemons and add it to the syrup.

By hand: Strain the syrup into a shallow freezerproof container, reserving the rind. Freeze the mixture for 4 hours until it is mushy.

Using an ice cream maker: Strain the syrup and lemon juice and churn the mixture until thick.

By hand: Scoop the sorbet into a food processor and beat it until smooth. Lightly whisk the egg white with a fork until it is just frothy. Spoon the sorbet back into the tub, beat in the egg white and return the mixture to the freezer for 4 hours.

Using an ice cream maker: Add the egg white to the mixture and continue to churn for 10–15 minutes until firm enough to scoop.

Scoop into bowls or glasses and decorate with sugared lemon rind.

LEMON MOUSSE

Light and airy, this heavenly dessert is also easy to make and refreshing. To add extra texture crumble macaroons into the bottom of the dessert glasses and pour the mousse over them.

Serves 6

50ml/2fl oz/¼ cup apple juice
    or water
30ml/2 tbsp powdered gelatine
15ml/1 tbsp grated lemon zest
90ml/6 tbsp fresh lemon juice
4 eggs, separated
175g/6oz icing (confectioner's)
    sugar
250ml/8fl oz/1 cup double
    (heavy) cream
strips of lemon julienne, to
    garnish

Pour the apple juice or water into a small bowl. Add the gelatine until softened. Add 120ml/4fl oz/½ cup boiling water and stir to dissolve the gelatine, then stir in the lemon zest and juice.

Combine the egg yolks with 150g/5oz of the icing sugar in a bowl, and beat until frothy. Fold the gelatine mixture into the egg yolks. Refrigerate for at least 1 hour. Beat the egg whites until stiff and fold them into the egg yolk mixture.

Beat the cream until stiff peaks form, and stir in the remaining icing sugar. Fold half the cream into the egg and lemon mixture.

Spoon the mousse into a deep, 2 litre/3½ pint glass bowl or 6 individual bowls. Chill until set. Serve decorated with the remaining whipped cream and lemon julienne.

Energy 278kcal/1159kJ; Protein 3.7g; Carbohydrate 23.4g, of which sugars 23.4g; Fat 19.6g, of which saturates 11.2g; Cholesterol 138mg; Calcium 41mg; Fibre 0g; Sodium 43mg.

NOTE
Raw eggs are not recommended for very young children and pregnant women.

SURPRISE LEMON PUDDING

Although all the ingredients are mixed together, during cooking a tangy lemon sauce forms beneath a light topping, making this lemon pudding a tasty surprise.

Serves 4

75g/3oz/6 tbsp unsalted (sweet) butter
175g/6oz/¾ cup soft light brown sugar
4 eggs, separated
grated zest and juice of 4 lemons
50g/2oz/½ cup self-raising (self-rising) flour
120ml/4fl oz/½ cup milk
icing (confectioners') sugar, to decorate

COOK'S TIP

When whisking egg whites, use a grease-free bowl and make sure that there are no traces of yolk.

Preheat the oven to 180°C/350°F/Gas 4. Butter an 18cm/7in soufflé dish and stand it in a roasting pan (tin).

Beat the butter and sugar together in a large bowl until pale and very fluffy. Beat in one egg yolk at a time, beating well after each addition and gradually beating in the lemon zest and juice until well mixed; do not worry if the mixture curdles a little.

Sift the flour and stir it into the lemon mixture until well mixed, then gradually stir in the milk.

Whisk the egg whites in a separate bowl until stiff, but not dry, then lightly, but thoroughly, fold into the lemon mixture in three batches. Carefully pour the mixture into the soufflé dish, then pour boiling water into the roasting pan.

Bake the pudding in the middle of the oven for approximately 45 minutes, or until golden on top. Dust with icing (confectioners') sugar and serve immediately.

Energy 319kcal/3131kJ; Protein 12.1g;
Carbohydrate 58.1g, of which sugars 35.5g;
Fat 53.2g, of which saturates 27g;
Cholesterol 185mg; Calcium 282mg;
Fibre 3.9g; Sodium 304mg

LEMON DROPS

Adorable miniature lemon-shaped drops are a classic sweet around the world. Opaque yellow with a sugary coating, they have a certain sparkle and make perfect gifts.

Makes about 600g/1lb 6oz
grapeseed or groundnut
(peanut) oil, for greasing
400g/14oz/2 cups caster
(superfine) sugar, plus
200g/7oz/1 cup for dusting
15ml/1 tbsp liquid glucose
150ml/¼ pint/²⁄₃ cup water
2.5ml/½ tsp lemon oil or 5ml/1
tsp lemon extract
2 drops yellow food colouring

COOK'S TIP
These lemon drops can be served immediately, or wrapped in baking parchment and stored in an airtight container.

Energy 2412kcal/10289kJ; Protein 3g;
Carbohydrate 639.7g, of which sugars
633g; Fat 0g, of which saturates 0g;
Cholesterol 0mg; Calcium 319mg;
Fibre 0g; Sodium 59mg.

Grease a marble slab, metal scraper and some kitchen scissors. Prepare an ice-water bath.

Combine the sugar, liquid glucose and water in a medium, heavy pan and bring to the boil. Reduce the heat to medium and cook, without stirring, until the mixture reaches the soft-crack stage (143°C/290°F). Remove the pan from the heat and stir in the lemon oil or extract and yellow food colouring. Stir until the mixture stops bubbling. Arrest the cooking by placing the pan in the ice-water bath.

Pour the syrup on to the oiled marble slab and allow it to cool until a skin forms. Using the oiled scraper, begin to fold the edges into the centre of the pool until it is cool enough to handle. Oil your hands and, using the scraper, lift the syrup up off the marble and work it into a cylindrical shape. Pull it out from either end to make a long strand.

Take hold of the ends of the syrup strand and pull them up towards you to form a 'U' shape. Twist the two sides together into a rope, then pull again from both ends to make the 'U' shape.

Repeat these steps for about 15–20 minutes, until the syrup rope becomes opaque and a lot lighter in colour. You need to keep working it constantly so that it remains supple. If it becomes too hard, you can put it in a cool oven for a few minutes until it softens enough to work.

Gently pull the syrup into a long, thin strand again, then fold it in half and then in half again so that you have four even lengths. Twist these up into an even rope and pull until the diameter is about 2cm/1in.

Use the oiled scissors to cut the pulled syrup into small, even pieces. Roll the pieces into little ovals between your oiled hands.

Pinch each end into a point to make them look like lemons. Place the caster sugar in a bowl and toss in the lemon drops to coat.

INDEX